NATEF Correlated Task Sheets

for

Automotive Heating and Air Conditioning

Seventh Edition

James D. Halderman

Tom Birch

PEARSON

Boston Columbus Indianapolis New York San Francisco Hoboken
Amsterdam Cape Town Dubai London Madrid Milan Munich Paris Montreal Toronto
Delhi Mexico City Sao Paulo Sydney Hong Kong Seoul Singapore Taipei Tokyo

Product Manager: Lindsey Prudhomme Gill
Program Manager: Holly Shufeldt
Project Manager: Rex Davidson
Editorial Assistant: Nancy Kesterson
Team Lead Project Manager: JoEllen Gohr
Team Lead Program Manager: Laura Weaver
Director of Marketing: David Gesell
Senior Marketing Coordinator: Stacey Martinez
Senior Marketing Assistant: Les Roberts
Procurement Specialist: Deidra M. Skahill
Media Project Manager: Noelle Chun
Media Project Coordinator: April Cleland
Cover Designer: Integra Software Services, Ltd.
Creative Director: Andrea Nix
Art Director: Diane Y. Ernsberger
Full-Service Project Management and Composition:
  Integra Software Services, Ltd.
Printer/Binder: LSC Communications
Cover Printer: LSC Communications.

2 16

ISBN-10:   0-13-351535-4
ISBN-13: 978-0-13-351535-0

Table of Contents

Chapter 11 – Heating System Operation and Diagnosis

Chapter 12 – Automatic Temperature Control Systems

Chapter 13 – Hybrid and Electric Vehicle HVAC Systems

Chapter 14 – Refrigerant Recovery, Recycling, and Recharging

Chapter 15 – A/C System Diagnosis and Repair

Air Conditioning Work Order

Meets NATEF Task: (A7-A-2) Complete work order and complete necessary customer and vehicle information. (P-1)

Name _____ Date _____ Time on Task _____

Make/Model _____ Year _____ Evaluation: 4 3 2 1

_____ 1. List the items about the **vehicle** that should be included on the work order (also called a repair order - R.O).

      a. _____   e. _____

      b. _____   f. _____

      c. _____   g. _____

      d. _____   h. _____

_____ 2. List the information about the **driver/owner** that should be included on the work order.

      a. _____

      b. _____

      c. _____

      d. _____

_____ 3. List the three Cs (concern, cause, and correction) that the service technician should write on the work order for a repair that includes a diagnosis of the problem (concern), the replacement of a part, and the verification of the repair.

      a. _____

      b. _____

      c. _____

Material Safety Data Sheet (MSDS)

Meets NATEF Task: Not specified by NATEF

Name _____ **Date** _____ **Time on Task** _____

Make/Model _____ **Year** _____ **Evaluation: 4   3   2   1**

_____ **1.** Locate the MSDS sheets and describe their location _____

_____

_____ **2.** Select three commonly used chemicals or solvents. Record the following information from the MSDS:

• **Product name** _____

        chemical name(s) _____

        Does the chemical contain "chlor" or "fluor" which may indicate hazardous

        materials?   **Yes** _____   **No** _____

        flash point = _____ (hopefully above 140° F)

        pH _____ (7 = neutral, higher than 7 = caustic (base), lower than 7 = acid)

• **Product name** _____

        chemical name(s) _____

        Does the chemical contain "chlor" or "fluor" which may indicate hazardous

        materials?   **Yes** _____   **No** _____

        flash point = _____ (hopefully above 140° F)

        pH _____ (7 = neutral, higher than 7 = caustic (base), lower than 7 = acid)

• **Product name** _____

        chemical name(s) _____

        Does the chemical contain "chlor" or "fluor" which may indicate hazardous

        materials?   **Yes** _____   **No** _____

        flash point = _____ (hopefully above 140° F)

    pH _____ (7 = neutral, higher than 7 = caustic (base), lower than 7 = acid)

AC Component Identification

Meets NATEF Task: (None specified)

Name _____ **Date** _____ **Time on Task** _____

Make/Model _____ **Year** _____ **Evaluation:** 4 3 2 1

_____ **1.** Locate the air-conditioning system label. Describe the location.

_____

_____ **2.** According to the label, what type of refrigerant is used in the vehicle?

       _____ HFC-134a (R-134a or SUVA®)

       _____ CFC-12 (R-12 or Freon®)

_____ **3.** According to the label, what is the capacity of the system?

       _____ ounces

_____ **4.** Describe the location of the **compressor** _____

_____

_____ **5.** Describe the location of the **condenser** _____

_____

_____ **6.** Describe the location of the **evaporator** _____

_____

_____ **7.** Describe the location of the **accumulator** or **receiver-drier** _____

_____

_____ **8.** Does the system use an expansion valve?   _____ Yes _____ No

_____ **9.** Does the system use an orifice tube?   _____ Yes _____ No

HIGH TEMPERATURE AND HIGH PRESSURE
LOW TEMPERATURE AND LOW PRESSURE

LOW PRESSURE GAS   HIGH PRESSURE GAS

SUCTION LINE   DISCHARGE LINE

COMPRESSOR

EVAPORATOR   CONDENSER

OIL

TEMPERATURE SENSOR

LOW PRESSURE LIQUID   LIQUID LINE

THERMOSTATIC EXPANSION VALVE (TXV)   RECEIVER-DRIER →

HIGH PRESSURE LIQUID

HIGH TEMPERATURE AND HIGH PRESSURE
LOW TEMPERATURE AND LOW PRESSURE

LOW PRESSURE GAS   HIGH PRESSURE GAS

SUCTION LINE   DISCHARGE LINE

COMPRESSOR

ACCUMULATOR   EVAPORATOR   CONDENSER

OIL

LOW PRESSURE LIQUID   LIQUID LINE

ORIFICE TUBE

HIGH PRESSURE LIQUID

A/C Component Purpose and Function

Meets NATEF Task: None specified.

Name _____ Date _____ Time on Task _____

Make/Model _____ Year _____ Evaluation: 4 3 2 1

_____ **1.** Describe the purpose and function of the A/C compressor. _____

_____

_____

![Cutaway photo of an A/C compressor]

_____ **2.** Describe the purpose and function of the condenser. _____

_____

_____

_____ **3.** Describe the purpose and function of the thermal expansion valve (TXV). _____

_____

_____

_____ **4.** Describe the purpose and function of the orifice tube (OT). _____

_____

_____

_____ **5.** Describe the purpose and function of the evaporator. _____

_____

_____

A/C Compressor Clutch Control Diagnosis

Meets NATEF Task: (A7-D-2) Test and diagnose A/C compressor clutch control system; determine necessary action. (P-1)

Name _____ Date _____ Time on Task _____

Make/Model _____ Year _____ Evaluation: 4 3 2 1

_____ **1.** Check service information and determine the testing and diagnostic procedures to follow when diagnosing faults in the A/C compressor clutch control circuit (describe tests).

_____

_____

_____ **2.** What test equipment is specified for use during the diagnosis? Check all that apply.

    _____ a. DMM

    _____ b. Scope

    _____ c. Scan tool

    _____ d. Special tester (describe) _____

    _____ e. Other (describe) _____

_____ **3.** After testing the A/C compressor clutch circuit, what is the necessary action?

_____

Air Conditioning Compressor Service

Meets NATEF Task: (A7-B-2, A7-B-3, A7-B-6) Inspect and replace A/C compressor drive belt(s); determine necessary cause. (P-1, P-2, P-1)

Name _____ Date _____ Time on Task _____

Make/Model _____ Year _____ Evaluation: 4 3 2 1

_____ **1.** Check service information and list the inspection and replacement procedures for the

A/C compressor drive belt clutch and replacement. _____

_____

_____

_____ **2.** What is the specified method to use to determine the quantity of refrigerant oil? _____

_____

_____

_____ **3.** Inspect lines and fittings (describe) _____

_____ **4.** Based on the inspection, what is the necessary action? _____

_____

Refrigerant Oil Inspection

Meets NATEF Task: (A7-A-7, A7-A-8) Inspect condition of the refrigerant oil removed from the A/C system/ determine necessary action. (P-2, P-1)

Name _____ Date _____ Time on Task _____

Make/Model _____ Year _____ Evaluation: 4 3 2 1

_____ 1. Recover the refrigerant oil during the evacuation procedure.

_____ 2. How much oil was recovered? _____

_____ 3. Visually check the condition of the oil. Describe the condition: _____

_____

_____

_____ 4. What type of oil and viscosity is specified to be used?

Type = _____

Viscosity = _____

_____ 5. Based on your inspection, what is the necessary action? _____

_____

_____

Refrigerant Handling Equipment

Meets NATEF Task: (A7-E-1) Perform correct use and maintenance of refrigerant handling equipment. (P-1)

Name _____ Date _____ Time on Task _____

Make/Model _____ Year _____ Evaluation: 4 3 2 1

_____ **1.** What brand and type of refrigerant handling equipment is being used (describe)?

_____

_____

_____

_____ **2.** Check the instructions for the equipment and list the maintenance items that should be performed.

_____

_____

_____

_____ **3.** Check the instructions and describe how to properly use the refrigerant handling equipment. _____

_____

_____

Inspect the Air Conditioning Condenser

Meets NATEF Task: (A7-B-7) Inspect A/C condenser for airflow restriction; perform
necessary action. (P-1)

Name _____ Date _____ Time on Task _____

Make/Model _____ Year _____ Evaluation: 4 3 2 1

_____ 1. Check service information on how to gain access to the front side of the condenser
(describe what needs to be done). _____

_____

_____

_____ 2. What is the recommended method and/or tools needed to clean the condenser?

_____

_____

_____

_____ 3. Based on the inspection, what is the necessary action? _____

_____

_____

Receiver/Drier Accumulator Drier

Meets NATEF Task: (A7-B-8) Remove, inspect, and reinstall drier assembly; determine required oil quantity. (P-1)

Name _____ Date _____ Time on Task _____

Make/Model _____ Year _____ Evaluation: 4 3 2 1

_____ 1. Check service information for the procedure and tools needed to remove the drier

assembly. _____

_____

_____

_____

_____ 2. Check service information and determine the required amount of oil needed to be

added to the system if the drier assembly is replaced. _____ oz.

_____ 3. What was the condition of the removed drier assembly? _____

_____

_____

Replace Expansion Valve/Orifice Tube

Meets NATEF Task: (A7-B-9) Remove and install expansion valve or orifice tube.
(P-1)

Name _____ Date _____ Time on Task _____

Make/Model _____ Year _____ Evaluation: 4 3 2 1

_____ **1.** Check service information for the exact procedures to follow when replacing the
expansion valve or orifice tube. _____

_____

_____

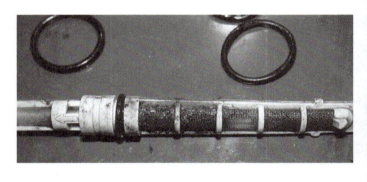

_____ **2.** List the tools needed to perform the removal and installation of the expansion valve or
orifice tube.

a. _____   d. _____   g. _____

b. _____   e. _____   h. _____

c. _____   f. _____   i. _____

Blower Motor Diagnosis

Meets NATEF Task: (A7-D-1) Inspect and test A/C blower motor and circuit; perform necessary action. (P-1)

Name _____ Date _____ Time on Task _____

Make/Model _____ Year _____ Evaluation: 4 3 2 1

_____ **1.** Locate the blower motor schematic and determine the following information:

    A. Describe the location _____

    B. Is the blower motor accessible from inside the vehicle or from under the hood?

    _____

    C. List the wire colors and their gauge:

        Power = _____

        Ground = _____

_____ **2.** List the specified testing procedure: _____

    _____

    _____

_____ **3.** How are the various speeds controlled?

    _____ Resistor pack

    _____ Electronic controller

    _____ Other (describe) _____

_____ **4.** What fuse number (label) and amperage rating are used for the blower motor?

    A. Fuse number (label) _____

    B. Fuse rating _____

_____ **5.** Describe the location of the ground(s) for the blower motor circuit. _____

    _____

_____ **6.** Measure the current draw of the blower motor on high speed.

    Amperage = _____ (normal blower motor amperage draw is about 12-14

    amperes)

_____ **7.** Based on the test results, what is the necessary action? _____

A/C and Heater Controls

Meets NATEF Task: (A7-D-3, A7-D-4, A7-D-5) Inspect and diagnose malfunctions with HVAC controls. (P-2, P-3, P-3)

Name _____ **Date** _____ **Time on Task** _____

Make/Model _____ **Year** _____ **Evaluation: 4 3 2 1**

_____ 1. Check for proper operation of the vacuum, mechanical, and electrical components and controls of the HVAC system. Describe the operation and/or faults detected.

_____

_____

_____

_____ 2. Check the operation of the A/C heater control panel assembly. Describe the operation and/or faults detected. _____

_____

_____ 3. Check the operation of the AC heater control cables (if equipped) and motors. Describe the operation and/or faults detected. _____

_____

_____ 4. Based on the inspection, what is the necessary action? _____

_____

_____

_____

HVAC Electrical Controls

Meets NATEF Task: (A7-D-1) Diagnose malfunctions in the HVAC electrical controls; determine necessary action. (P-2)

Name _____ Date _____ Time on Task _____

Make/Model _____ Year _____ Evaluation: 4 3 2 1

_____ **1.** Check service information and describe the specified procedures to follow to diagnose HVAC electrical control faults. _____

_____

_____

_____ **2.** Check all of the test equipment specified that is needed to diagnose HVAC electrical control faults.

_____ a. DMM

_____ b. Scan tool

_____ c. Special tester (describe) _____

_____ d. Other (describe) _____

_____ **3.** After diagnosis following the specified procedures, what is the necessary action?

_____

_____

Cooling System Inspection

Meets NATEF Task: (A7-C-1) Perform cooling system pressure tests; perform necessary action. (P-1)

Name _____ Date _____ Time on Task _____

Make/Model _____ Year _____ Evaluation: **4 3 2 1**

_____ 1. Check the level of coolant in the coolant recovery tank. It should be between the "full hot" and "full cold" lines.

        OK_____   **NOT OK**_____

_____ 2. After the engine has cooled, remove the radiator cap.

> **CAUTION:** Do not remove the radiator cap if the engine is hot. The coolant will explosively expand when the cap is removed which can cause severe burns to anyone near the vehicle.

_____ 3. The coolant should be at the full level in the radiator.

        OK_____   **NOT OK**_____

_____ 4. Check the freezing point and boiling point of the coolant.

        Freezing point = _____ [should be -34° F (-36° C) or lower]
        Boiling point = _____

        OK_____   **NOT OK**_____

_____ 5. Pressure test the cooling system by installing a cooling system pressure tester and pump until the pressure is equal to the pressure cap value. Pressure should hold if there are no leaks.

        OK_____   **NOT OK**_____

_____ 6. Test the radiator cap using the cooling system pressure tester with an adapter that fits the cap. The cap should hold its rated pressure.

        OK_____   **NOT OK**_____

_____ 7. What is the necessary action? _____

Heating System Performance Check

Meets NATEF Task: (A7-A-1, A7-C-2) Diagnose temperature control problems; determine necessary action. (P-2)

Name _____ Date _____ Time on Task _____

Make/Model _____ Year _____ Evaluation: 4 3 2 1

_____ **1.** Check the front of the radiator and air-conditioning condenser for debris that could

limit airflow. Clean as required.

        OK_____   **NOT OK_____**

_____ **2.** Perform a thorough visual inspection of the cooling system. Look for hoses that may

be leaking, cut, or swollen.

        OK_____   **NOT OK_____**

_____ **3.** Start the engine and operate the heater and air-conditioning controls for proper

operation including:

      defroster (airflow to windshield)   **OK_____**   **NOT OK_____**

      heater (airflow to floor)   **OK_____**   **NOT OK_____**

      A/C (airflow to vents)   **OK_____**   **NOT OK_____**

      blower motor on all speeds   **OK_____**   **NOT OK_____**

_____ **4.** Using an infrared pyrometer, measure the temperature of the upper radiator hose.

Temperature = _____ (should be close to the same temperature as the

thermostat rating)

        OK_____   **NOT OK_____**

_____ **5.** Based on the test results, what is the necessary action? _____

_____

17

Heater System Service

Meets NATEF Task: (A7-C-3, A7-C-4) Inspect and test heater control valve(s); perform necessary action. (P-2) / Remove heater core. (P-3)

Name _____ Date _____ Time on Task _____

Make/Model _____ Year _____ Evaluation: 4 3 2 1

_____ **1.** Check service information for the specified procedures to follow to test the heater control valves. _____

_____

_____

_____ **2.** Based on the inspection of the heater control valve(s), what is the necessary action?

_____

_____

_____

_____ **3.** Remove and install heater core as needed. _____

_____

18

A/C Ducts and Doors

Meets NATEF Task: (A7-C-3, A7-D-6) Diagnose temperature control problems in the heating system and determine procedures. (P-2)

Name _____ Date _____ Time on Task _____

Make/Model _____ Year _____ Evaluation: 4 3 2 1

_____ **1.** Check the operation of the heating and ventilation system. Describe the operation and/or faults detected. _____

_____

_____

_____ **2.** Based on the inspection, what is the necessary action? _____

_____

_____

19

Automatic/Dual Climate System ID

Meets NATEF Task: (A7-A-2) Research vehicle and service information. (P-1)

Name _____ Date _____ Time on Task _____

Make/Model _____ Year _____ Evaluation: 4 3 2 1

_____ 1. Check service information and identify the type of automatic or dual climate system

and check all that apply:

_____ automatic system

_____ dual climate system

_____ semi-automatic system

_____ 2. Check service information and determine what sensors are being used and where they

are located.

a. Ambient air temperature sensor; location _____

b. Evaporator outlet temperature sensor; location _____

c. Passenger component temperature sensor; location _____

d. Sunload sensor; location _____

e. Other (describe) _____; location _____

_____ 3. Describe the location of the other major components of the system.

Compressor(s); location _____

Evaporator(s); location _____

Blower motor(s); location _____

20

Automatic AC System Operation

Meets NATEF Task: (A7-A-9, A7-D-8) Check operation of automatic HVAC system; determine necessary action. (P-3)

Name _____ Date _____ Time on Task _____

Make/Model _____ Year _____ Evaluation: 4 3 2 1

_____ **1.** Check service information for the specified procedures to follow to inspect and test the A/C system operation. Describe the procedures. _____

_____

_____

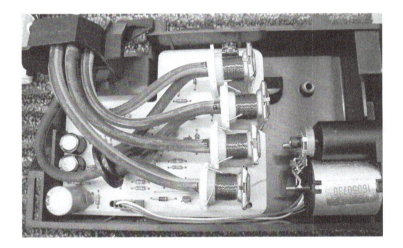

_____ **2.** What test equipment was specified to test the A/C system operation? Check all that apply.

     _____ a. DMM

     _____ b. Scan tool

     _____ c. Special tester (describe) _____

     _____ d. Other (describe) _____

_____ **3.** Based on the test results, what is the necessary action? _____

_____

21

Hybrid Vehicle A/C System Precautions

Meets NATEF Task: (A7-B-4) Identify hybrid vehicle A/C system electrical circuits, service, and safety precautions. (P-3)

Name _____ Date _____ Time on Task _____

Make/Model _____ Year _____ Evaluation: 4 3 2 1

_____ **1.** Check service information for the vehicle manufacturer's specified safety precautions regarding the A/C system electrical circuits, safety, and service.

A. Electrical circuit precautions:

_____

_____

_____

_____

_____

B. Safety precautions: _____

_____

_____

C. Service precautions: _____

_____

_____

_____

_____

_____

22

Hybrid A/C System Circuits

Meets NATEF Task: (A7-B-4) Identify hybrid vehicle A/C system circuits and safety precautions. (P-3)

Name _____ Date _____ Time on Task _____

Make/Model _____ Year _____ Evaluation: 4 3 2 1

_____ **1.** Check service information for the specified A/C system electrical circuits precautions.

_____

_____

_____ **2.** What is the part number of the specified refrigerant oil that should be used when servicing the air conditioning system?

_____

_____ **3.** List the A/C service procedures that can be performed. _____

_____

_____

23

Identify and Recover Refrigerant

Meets NATEF Task: (A7-E-1, A7-E-2) Identify and recover the air conditioning system refrigerant. (P-1)

Name _____ Date _____ Time on Task _____

Make/Model _____ Year _____ Evaluation: 4 3 2 1

_____ **1.** Check the instructions for the refrigerant identifying unit and describe the

recommended procedure. _____

_____

_____

_____ **2.** What did the identifying unit indicate was in the A/C system? _____

> **CAUTION:** If contaminated, do not recover the refrigerant unless a separate container is used for the contaminated refrigerant.

_____ **3.** Following the equipment manufacturer's instructions, recover the A/C system

refrigerant.

_____ **4.** How much refrigerant was recovered? _____

_____ **5.** How much oil was recovered? _____

24

Recycle Refrigerant

Meets NATEF Task: (A7-E-3) Recycle the refrigerant. (P-1)

Name _____ Date _____ Time on Task _____

Make/Model _____ Year _____ Evaluation: 4 3 2 1

_____ **1.** Check the operating instructions for the recycling machine and describe the

procedures specified. _____

_____

_____

_____

_____ **2.** How many ounces were recycled? _____

_____ **3.** What cautions or warnings were included in the instructions? _____

_____

_____

_____

_____

25

Evacuate and Charge A/C System

Meets NATEF Task: (A7-E-4) Evacuate and charge air conditioning system.
(P-1)

Name _____ Date _____ Time on Task _____

Make/Model _____ Year _____ Evaluation: 4 3 2 1

_____ **1.** Check the underhood decal or A/C pressure fittings to verify the type of refrigerant that should be in the system. CFC-12 ___ HFC-134a ___ other _____

_____ **2.** Connect an A/C refrigerant identification to the fitting and determine the type of refrigerant that is in the system. CFC-12 ___ HFC-134a ___ other _____
(Do not proceed with the recovery unless the refrigerant is properly identified.)

_____ **3.** Connect the hoses from the recovery unit to both the high-side and low-side fittings.

_____ **4.** Recover the refrigerant and note the amount of refrigerant oil that was removed from the system. Amount of refrigerant oil recovered = _____

_____ **5.** Repair any leaks in the system and/or replace any failed component.

> **NOTE:** Most vehicle manufacturers recommend replacing the accumulator or receiver drier if the system has been open for any length of time or if the compressor has failed.

_____ **6.** Evacuate the system to a vacuum of at least 27" Hg (best if 29" Hg) for at least 45 minutes.

Lowest vacuum level reached = _____ Time spent evacuating = _____

_____ **7.** Recharge the system with the specified amount of refrigerant.

_____ **8.** Start the engine and check the high-side and the low-side pressures:

low-side pressure = _____ high-side pressure = _____

_____ **9.** Check the temperature of the air from the center air-conditioning vent.

Air temperature = _____ [should be 35° - 45° F (2° - 7° C)]

OK_____   NOT OK_____

26

Air-Conditioning System Performance Test

Meets NATEF Task: (A7-A-1, A7-A-3) Performance test the A/C system and diagnose using principles of refrigeration. (P-1)

Name _____ Date _____ Time on Task _____

Make/Model _____ Year _____ Evaluation: 4 3 2 1

> **NOTE:** This test procedure is best performed when the temperature is above 70° F (21° C).

_____ 1. Start the engine, turn the air conditioning to maximum cooling, open the doors and windows, and increase engine speed to about 1500-2000 RPM.

_____ 2. Turn the blower motor to high speed.

_____ 3. Measure the temperature of the air at the air-conditioning vent in the center of the dash.

   Temperature = _____ [should be 35° - 45° F (2° - 7° C)]

   OK_____   NOT OK_____

_____ 4. Stop the engine and visually inspect the condition of the air-conditioning compressor drive belt (accessory drive belt).

   OK_____   NOT OK_____

_____ 5. Visually check for any signs of leaking refrigerant oil that could indicate a refrigerant leak.

   OK_____   NOT OK_____

27

Air Conditioning Noise Diagnosis

Meets NATEF Task: (A7-A-4) Diagnose abnormal operating noise; determine necessary action. (P-2)

Name _____ Date _____ Time on Task _____

Make/Model _____ Year _____ Evaluation: 4 3 2 1

_____ 1. Check service information for the suggested method and procedures to follow when

   diagnosing abnormal noise concerns (describe procedure): _____

   _____

   _____

_____ 2. Describe the noise (check all that apply):

   _____ a. Under the hood

   _____ b. Inside the passenger compartment

   _____ c. Wind noise

   _____ d. Rattle

   _____ e. Shriek

   _____ f. Squeal

   _____ Other (describe): _____

_____ 3. After diagnosis of the noise using the recommended procedures, what is the necessary

   action? _____

   _____

   _____

28

Refrigerant Identification/Read Pressures

Meets NATEF Task: (A7-A-5) Identify refrigerant type; connect the gauges and read the pressures. (P-1)

Name _____ **Date** _____ **Time on Task** _____

Make/Model _____ **Year** _____ **Evaluation: 4   3   2   1**

_____ **1.** Read, understand, and follow the instructions for the refrigerant identification machine

and determine the type of refrigerant in the system.

Type: _____

Contaminated? Yes _____   No _____ If yes, state the results of the test:

_____

_____ **2.** Connect the gauges as per the equipment manufacturer's instructions:

Low pressure = _____

High pressure = _____

29

Leak Test the Air Conditioning System

Meets NATEF Task: (A7-A-6) Leak test the air conditioning system; determine necessary action. (P-1)

Name _____ Date _____ Time on Task _____

Make/Model _____ Year _____ Evaluation: 4 3 2 1

_____ 1. Check service information and describe the leak detection recommended by the

vehicle manufacturer. _____

_____

_____ 2. What type(s) of leak detection tools or equipment was used (describe)? _____

_____

_____ 3. Was a leak detected? Yes _____ No _____ If yes, describe the location: _____

_____

_____ 4. Based on the test results, what is the necessary action? _____

_____

30

Determine Need for Refrigerant Filter

Meets NATEF Task: (A7-B-5) Determine the need for an additional A/C system filter; perform necessary action. (P-3)

Name _____ Date _____ Time on Task _____

Make/Model _____ Year _____ Evaluation: 4 3 2 1

_____ 1. Check service information and determine when the vehicle manufacturer recommends the installation of an additional filter in the refrigerant system. _____

_____

_____

_____ 2. Check aftermarket information and determine when an additional filter is recommended to be installed. _____

_____

_____

_____

_____

_____

_____

_____ 3. Where is an additional filter installed? (describe the location) _____

_____

_____ 4. Why is the filter installed in this location? _____

_____

_____

_____ 5. What was the necessary action? _____

_____

_____

31

AC System Performance Check

Meets NATEF Task: (A7-B-11) Perform test of air conditioning system. (P-1)

Name _____ Date _____ Time on Task _____

Make/Model _____ Year _____ Evaluation: 4 3 2 1

NOTE: This test procedure is best performed when the temperature is above 70° F (21° C).

_____ **1.** Start the engine, turn the air conditioning to maximum cooling, open the doors and windows, and increase engine speed to about 1500-2000 RPM.

_____ **2.** Turn the blower motor to high speed.

_____ **3.** Measure the temperature of the air at the air-conditioning vent in the center of the dash.

        Temperature = _____ [should be 35° - 45° F (2° - 7° C)]

        OK_____   **NOT OK_____**

_____ **4.** Stop the engine and visually inspect the condition of the air-conditioning compressor drive belt (accessory drive belt).

        OK_____   **NOT OK_____**

_____ **5.** Visually check for any signs of leaking refrigerant oil that could indicate a refrigerant leak.

        OK_____   **NOT OK_____**

32

AC System Diagnosis

Meets NATEF Task: (A7-B-11) Perform test of air conditioning system. (P-1)

Name _____ Date _____ Time on Task _____

Make/Model _____ Year _____ Evaluation: 4 3 2 1

_____ **1.** Measure and record the ambient air temperature and relative humidity.

      ambient air temperature = _____

      relative humidity = _____

_____ **2.** Start the engine, turn the air conditioning to maximum cooling, open the doors and windows, and increase engine speed to about 1500-2000 RPM.

_____ **3.** Turn the blower motor to high speed.

_____ **4.** Measure the temperature of the air at the air-conditioning vent in the center of the dash.

      Temperature = _____ [should be 30 degrees F cooler than ambient]

      OK_____   **NOT OK**_____

_____ **5.** Check service information and compare the results of the measurements to factory specification.

      OK_____   **NOT OK**_____

33

Identify Source of A/C System Odors

Meets NATEF Task: (A7-D-7) Identify the source of A/C system odors. (P-1)

Name _____ Date _____ Time on Task _____

Make/Model _____ Year _____ Evaluation: 4   3   2   1

_____ 1. Check the vehicle for odors that are noticeable when the A/C system is operating.

Describe the odor. _____

_____

_____ 2. Check service information for the specified procedure to follow to eliminate the

source of the odor. Describe the specified procedure. _____

_____

_____

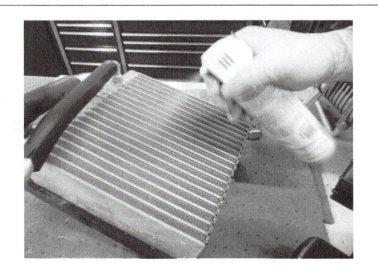

34

Evaporator Housing Drain

Meets NATEF Task: (A7-B-10) Inspect evaporator housing water drain; perform necessary action. (P-3)

Name _____ Date _____ Time on Task _____

Make/Model _____ Year _____ Evaluation: 4 3 2 1

_____ 1. Check service information to determine what the customer concern would be if the evaporator drain were clogged. _____

_____

_____

_____ 2. Check service information and determine the location of the evaporator drain describe the location). _____

_____

_____ 3. Inspect the drain. Was it clogged? **Yes** _____ **No** _____

_____ 4. Based on the inspection, what is the necessary action? _____

_____

35

Evaporator/Heater Core Replacement

Meets NATEF Task: (A7-B-12, A7-C-4) Remove, inspect, and reinstall evaporator; determine required oil quantity. (P-3)

Name _____ Date _____ Time on Task _____

Make/Model _____ Year _____ Evaluation: 4 3 2 1

_____ **1.** Check service information and determine the specified procedures to follow to replace the evaporator. (list the procedures)

a. _____   d. _____   g. _____

b. _____   e. _____   h. _____

c. _____   f. _____   i. _____

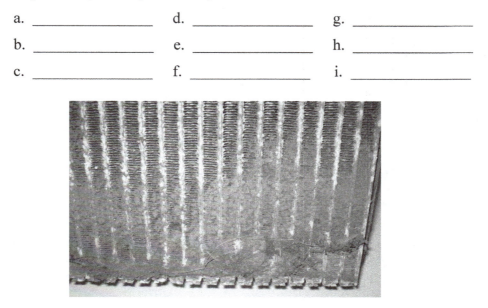

_____ **2.** Check service information and determine the amount of oil needed to add to the system when replacing the component.

Oil amount = _____ oz.

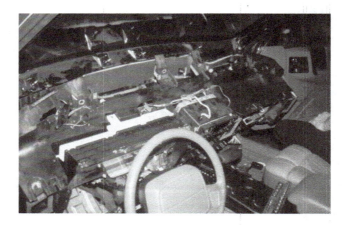

36

Condenser Replacement

Meets NATEF Task: (A7-B-13) Remove, inspect, and replace condenser; determine required oil quantity. (P-3)

Name _____ **Date** _____ **Time on Task** _____

Make/Model _____ **Year** _____ **Evaluation: 4 3 2 1**

_____ **1.** Check service information and determine the specified procedures to follow to replace the condenser. (list the procedures)

a. _____ d. _____ g. _____

b. _____ e. _____ h. _____

c. _____ f. _____ i. _____

_____ **2.** Check service information and determine the amount of oil needed to add to the system when replacing the component.

Oil amount = _____ oz.

Inspect Belts and Hoses

Meets NATEF Task: (A7-B-1) Inspect engine cooling and heating system hoses and belts; perform necessary action. (P-1)

Name _____ Date _____ Time on Task _____

Make/Model _____ Year _____ Evaluation: 4 3 2 1

_____ 1. Check service information for the procedures and specifications for determining the
condition of belts and hoses. _____
_____
_____

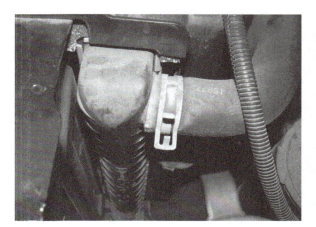 

_____ 2. Describe the condition of the heater hoses. _____
_____

_____ 3. Describe the condition of the radiator hoses. _____
_____

_____ 4. Describe the condition of the drive belt(s). _____
_____

_____ 5. Based on the inspection results, what is the necessary action? _____
_____
_____